Living The Fast Life:
The Ultimate Guide To Biblical Fasting

I.   Introduction

This guide is an expedition into the relationship of fasting and the Bible. As a Christian I believe that the Bible is the established and infallible Word of God. The majority of questions that we have about God and the Bible itself, can be answered by the Bible, whether directly or implied. Now, I did say the majority and not all questions can be answered. Somethings will not be revealed until we are in eternity and God reveals them to us.

However, topics like fasting can be known by studying and rightly dividing God's established word of Truth. This guide will attempt to answer any questions and bridge any gaps in your knowledge, understanding, and wisdom of Biblical fasting. And lift practical biblical strategies to successfully fast and receive all that God has for us in this DIVINE discipline.

II.   What Is fasting?

At the time of this writing, fasting is defined as "a willing abstinence or reduction from some or all food, drink, or both, for a period of time." An absolute fast or dry fasting, as it is called, is normally defined as abstaining from all foods and liquids for a fix period, usually a period of 24 hours, or a number of days. Water fasting allows drinking water but nothing else. Other fastings may be partially restrictive, limiting only particular foods or substances. A fast may also be intermittent in nature. Fasting practices may preclude intercourse and other activities as well as food.

III.   What Is Biblical Fasting?

Though the majority would define fasting as stated in the "What Is Fasting?" section of this guide, when we study the conditions surrounding the fasting accounts in the Bible, fasting is defined as a complete prohibition of all foods and liquids, meaning nothing would enter the mouth of the participant. The Bible doesn't teach directly, indirectly, or by revelation, that fasting has any other acceptable variations. The only fasting recognized in the Bible is what we call dry fasting. The complete abstinence from any food source or other sources to relieve hunger.

Based on Biblical study, God does not recognize any other types of abstinence as fasting. So, fasting from types of meats or other foods, from events, or even social media is not Biblically accepted as fasting. Though, when one is fasting, abstaining from social media and events tend to come with the territory, as we would want to devote as much time as possible intimately in the presence of God. We fast to deny and empty ourselves of ourselves, so that we may receive more of God. But, we will explore more deeply the Biblical reasons for fasting a little later in this guide.

Fasting is a natural discipline that can only be completed by the willingness of our Spirits. Jesus was lead into the wilderness by the Spirit of God, but He was not forced. He was willing to comply with the leading of the Holy Spirit, and as we will study later He had no food nor drink for 40 full days.

An interesting fact that should be pointed out, as stated before, fasting is a complete refusal from all foods & water. I reiterate this to point out that the Prophet Daniel did not fast when he and the three (3) Hebrew boys were taken captive. The four (4) Hebrew boys chose not to eat the "choice" or "fine" meats of king Nebuchadnezzar, because they had been offered up to his gods and the four (4) Hebrew boys did not want to dishonor their God and defile themselves by eating the defiled meats presented to them. The scriptural reference for this is found in the Bible in the Book of Daniel, chapter one (1), verses three (3) through twenty-one (21) [Daniel 1:3-21]. It has been taught that there is a "Daniel Fast", but again as defined Biblically, Daniel and the three (3) Hebrew boys did not abstain from food completely, but they refused to eat the defiled meats of Nebuchadnezzar in order to honor their God. Be sure to check out the "Ultimate List of Fasting Scriptures" section later in this guide.

Fast, Fasted, Fasting are defined in the Hebrew language as "to cover over (the mouth).", which further implies that if the mouth is covered, then nothing can enter the mouth, whether, food or drink. Below are the Strong's Concordance entries:

h6684 tsum: to abstain from food, fast
Original Word: צוּם
Part of Speech: Verb
Transliteration: tsum
Phonetic Spelling: (tsoom)
Short Definition: fasted

h6685 tsom: fasting, a fast
Original Word: צוֹם
Part of Speech: Noun Masculine
Transliteration: tsom
Phonetic Spelling: (tsome)
Short Definition: fast

Here are scriptures where found is a direct and contextual definition for fasting:

Esther 4:16 (NKJV)
"Go, gather all the Jews who are present in Shushan, and fast for me; neither eat nor drink for three (3) days, night or day. My maids and I will fast likewise..."

Psalm 109:24 (NKJV)
"my knees are weak through fasting, and my flesh is feeble from lack of fatness."

IV. Circumstances & Reasons Surrounding Fasting Found In The Bible

The Bible illustrates various reasons that the people in it fasted. Below you will find a list and brief explanations for the reasons illustrated in the Bible.

1. For direction: Judges 20:26-28

    The fast here was carried out so that the children of Israel could inquire of God if they should go out to battle against their cousin tribe, the tribe of Benjamin.

2. To confess sin and show sorrow of sinning against the Lord: 1 Samuel 7:3-6

    We see here that Israel had sinned against God and they were sorrowful for violating their covenant with God. To show that they were sorrow, they drew water and poured it out before God and denied their body of its desire.

3. In mourning: 2 Samuel 1:1-12

    David was so saddened by the news of the death of King Saul and his son Jonathan, that he and all his men tore their clothes, mourned, wept, and fasted because of the news.

4. Interceding: 2 Samuel 12:16

    In a desperate plea that God would spare his son conceived in sin, King David fasted in hopes that God would have mercy and spare his baby son. Fasting and prayer go hand in hand, however, realistically we can not expect God to honor our desperation in sin. There are many Biblical and modern cases of fasting and prayer that moves on the compassion of God in our favor, but the absolute variable condition is righteousness.

5. To humble oneself: Psalm 35:13

David used fasting as a tool to humble himself. While praying to God to defend him against his enemies, David wanted to make sure that although He was praying about someone else's wickedness, he himself was in alignment with God's heart. He fasted to humble himself that his own prayers against wickedness would penetrate his heart, so that he would not become what he was praying against.

6. For Divine discipline of self: Psalm 69:10

David at times would fast to discipline or chasten his soul when found in reproach against God. He did this so much that it was evident to everyone else when he had sinned against God.

7. For spiritual deliverance from demon possession: Mark 9:29

Jesus was asked by His disciples why they could not cast out the demon from the young boy. And Jesus revealed to them that on their part they needed to give themselves to fasting and prayer in order to overcome deeply rooted demons. (Please keep watch for "The Ultimate Guide on Spiritual Warfare" as we study being delivered from mental illnesses.)

8. To minister to God: Luke 2:37

Anna, the prophetess, was widowed for eighty-four (84) years and she spent that time ministering to God with fastings and prayers night and day.

9. To appoint for Spiritual Assignment: Acts 13:3

The prophets and teachers in the church at Antioch, after receiving instructions from the Holy Spirit, fasted, prayed, and laid hands on Barnabas, Saul to support and appoint them for ministry.

10. Fasting enduring suffering: 2 Corinthians 6:4

The ministry of Paul and his cohorts were proven because of their ability to remain faithful to fasting even in the midst of their sufferings.

Even though the list that precludes us covers the circumstances and reasons surrounding all fasts in the Bible, we will never be able to out do what has come directly from the mouth of God. Let's take a look at the reasons and benefits of fasting given by God Himself through the mouth of the Prophet Isaiah:

Isaiah 58:6-14 (NKJV)

[6] "*Is* this not the fast that I have chosen:
To loose the bonds of wickedness,
To undo the heavy burdens,
To let the oppressed go free,
And that you break every yoke?
[7] *Is it* not to share your bread with the hungry,
And that you bring to your house the poor who are cast out;
When you see the naked, that you cover him,
And not hide yourself from your own flesh?
[8] Then your light shall break forth like the morning,
Your healing shall spring forth speedily,
And your righteousness shall go before you;
The glory of the LORD shall be your rear guard.
[9] Then you shall call, and the LORD will answer;
You shall cry, and He will say, 'Here I *am*.'
"If you take away the yoke from your midst,
The pointing of the finger, and speaking wickedness,
[10] *If* you extend your soul to the hungry
And satisfy the afflicted soul,
Then your light shall dawn in the darkness,
And your darkness shall *be* as the noonday.
[11] The LORD will guide you continually,
And satisfy your soul in drought,
And strengthen your bones;
You shall be like a watered garden,
And like a spring of water, whose waters do not fail.

[12] Those from among you
Shall build the old waste places;
You shall raise up the foundations of many generations;
And you shall be called the Repairer of the Breach,
The Restorer of Streets to Dwell In.
[13] "If you turn away your foot from the Sabbath,
From doing your pleasure on My holy day,
And call the Sabbath a delight,
The holy *day* of the LORD honorable,
And shall honor Him, not doing your own ways,
Nor finding your own pleasure,
Nor speaking *your own* words,
[14] Then you shall delight yourself in the LORD;
And I will cause you to ride on the high hills of the earth,
And feed you with the heritage of Jacob your father.
The mouth of the LORD has spoken."

V.   Is Fasting Needed For Today's Christian?

Often is the question posed "is fasting is for the Christian today?". Many believe that because Christ died and He has sent the Holy Spirit to live within us, that there is no need to fast, because all power resides in us. While it is true that the Holy Spirit dwells in all Christians, it is also true that the benefits of fasting are only released by fasting.

Long after Jesus' death, the Apostles fasted. Not only did the Apostles fast, but they also instructed the church's to fast as well. The Apostles left behind examples of them fasting to seek the will of God, to discipline their flesh, to appoint leaders in the Church, to break satanic grips, etc. If the mighty men of God still observed the discipline of fasting it is safe to say it is for the modern Christian. How much more should we need to fast in our modern age compared to the age of the first (1st) century Church!

Today we are pulled in so many directions with our personal ambitions, fast-paced lives, and social media driven human interactions. There must be a way for today's Christian to remain righteous before God, seeking His will, and disciplining our fleshly desires. In comes fasting. Fasting is the vehicle to empty ourselves of all the junk that comes along with being in the world, but not being of it. It makes room for the Christian to be filled with the Glory of God (His Power and Presence).

Remember, God spoke through the Prophet Isaiah stating that fasting would loose the bonds of wickedness that try to infiltrate our lives. Whenever we find ourselves as Christians being bombarded with wicked thoughts and impulses, fasting will create the inward Spiritual environment that we need to have them loosened and us freed from them. We're promised that fasting will ensure us that we will realize Spiritual Victory over the enemy. (Isaiah 58:6)

In a world that teaches us to be selfish, fasting disciplines us to be thoughtful and giving, seeing to the needs of others who are in need. Fasting helps us as today's Christian not to be recluses only enjoying the blessings of God for ourselves. (Isaiah 58:7-8)

Fasting creates an environment within ourselves that allows for the Healing Power of God to flow through the believer, according to the will of God. When we find ourselves sick and attacked by disease, let us remember to fast that we may quickly receive healing according to the will of God. (Isaiah 58:8)

The Christian who disciplines himself to fast can be assured that the Power and Presence of God will not only lead them, but also follow them, alerting and protecting them from what he cannot see. Fasting gives the today's Christian Spiritual depth of sight in situations that otherwise seem okay and of the norm. (Isaiah 58:8)

Fasting is for the Christian of today, who desires to be naked before God, allowing God to reveal the things in our lives preventing us from being the Empowered Child of God He has called us to be. How great and powerful of an animal is an ox? But when an ox has been yoked with an ox-bow, it's power has now been reduced and even repurposed by it's dictator. Fasting allows for the

Glory of God to reign, rule, and function in the life of the Christian. (Isaiah 58:9-11)

Image of Ox-Bow:

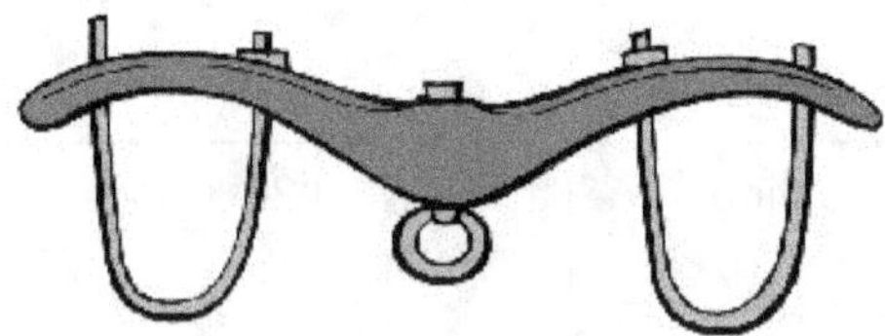

"image taken from https://assets2.cdn-mw.com/mw/static/art/dict/oxbow.gif"

Fasting will allow for the Christian of today to function as a reconciler of God for those individuals in our generation that do not know God. As we fast and seek the will of God, we position ourselves as Ambassadors of God to restore the world who has alienated itself from God. (Isaiah 58:12)

Fasting causes us not to find joy in our own selfish pleasures, but it allows us to delight ourselves in God by delighting in being made available to fulfill the will of God. Fasting releases the blessings and promises of God that we find only in being hidden in Jesus. (Isaiah 58:14)

VI. Different Types of Fasts Found In The Bible

As we have discovered what the actual Biblical fast is defined as, we can no longer come to the conclusion that for the Christian looking to please God through fasting can simply partake in just any fast expecting to accomplish this. But, by Biblical definition, there are not different types of fasting, but rather different lengths of fasting. I'd like to also mention that while there are different fast lengths lifted in scripture, there is no commandment from God whether direct or implied that there is a requirement of the length that we abstain from all food, water, and drinks to satisfy an expectation of God in fasting.

God directly and specifically spoke through the Prophet Isaiah decreeing that fasting is a complete denial of all food, drink, and water. But, nowhere in scripture is it revealed that God decreed a particular length of fasting. Please see the list below of fasting lengths and scriptures.

One (1) Day Fasting	Judges 20:26	Then all the children of Israel, that is, all the people, went up and came to the house of God and wept. They sat there before the LORD and fasted that day until evening; and they offered burnt offerings and peace offerings before the LORD.

Three (3) Day Fasting	Esther 4:16	"Go, gather all the Jews who are present in Shushan, and fast for me; neither eat nor drink for three days, night or day. My maids and I will fast likewise. And so I will go to the king, which *is* against the law; and if I perish, I perish!"

Seven (7) Day Fasting	1 Samuel 31:13	Then they took their bones and buried them under the tamarisk tree at Jabesh, and fasted seven days.

Forty (40) Day Fasting	Exodus 34:28	So he was there with the Lord forty days and forty nights. He neither ate bread nor drank water.

Forty (40) Day Fasting continued		And he wrote on the tablets the words of the covenant, the Ten Commandments.
	1 Kings 19:8	And he arose and ate and drank, and went in the strength of that food forty days and forty nights to Horeb, the mount of God.
	Matthew 4	Then Jesus was led up by the Spirit into the wilderness to be tempted by the devil. And after fasting forty days and forty nights, he was hungry.

Since there is no commandment on the length that a fast should be, we are left with the opportunity to choose the length of fasting. Fasting is an opportunity, not for the Christian to show God how much they need Him, but for a Christian to show himself how much he is in need of God.

VII. Should We Only Fast When We Are Led By The Holy Spirit?

It has been taught that we should only fast when we have been led by the Holy Spirit to do so. However, through surface and in depth study of the Bible, we see that not everyone who fasted was led by God to fast, but if there was a leading it was to do something else and fasting accompanied that assignment. For example, Jesus was led by the Holy Spirit not to fast, but into the wilderness to be tempted of the devil:

Matthew 4:1-2 (NKJV)

Then Jesus was led up by the Spirit into the wilderness to be tempted by the devil. And when He had fasted forty days and forty nights, afterward He was hungry.

Being led to do anything by the Holy Spirit is a sure way to please God and accomplish the assignments and purposes He sets before us. However, it is a Biblical fact that God is not sitting on His Throne with a master controller making Christians think and act. But, just like in the beginning account of existence itself and the creation of mankind, God made things with a purpose and abilities and He delights to see His creation develop and function as long as it does not rebel against Him and its purpose of existing. Oh, what joy it brings parents to see the once little baby to grow, develop, succeed, and exceed the instructions and knowledge they reared the child with. We can only image that that same feeling in multiplied times infinity with God.

VIII. How To Successfully Complete A Biblical Fast?

Spiritual success is only determined by God. It doesn't matter how well we think something is or went, but we must submit all of our ideologies to the Knowledge of God given to us by the sacred Scriptures. So, we turn to the only direct teaching on fasting found in the Bible. And that is the teaching given by Jesus to His disciples.

Matthew 6:16-18 (NKJV)

"Moreover, when you fast, do not be like the hypocrites, with a sad countenance. For they disfigure their faces that they may appear to men to be fasting. Assuredly, I say to you, they have their reward. But you, when you fast, anoint your head and wash your face, so that you do not appear to men to be fasting, but to your Father who *is* in the secret *place;* and your Father who sees in secret will reward you openly."

In the previous scriptures lifted, we see that Jesus did not say to the disciples if you fast, but He stated when you fast, implying that fasting is to be found in the life of His disciples, those individuals who give up their own identities in order to take on the image and identity of Jesus Christ. We now refer to these people as Christians. It is my prayer that if you are not identified as a Christian, that the only Spirit moves on you that you would submit your very being to God and repent and become a Christian.

Back to the lesson. Fasting is not a requirement in order to be a Christian. However, the Bible teaches us that it is a requirement in order for the Christian to fully realize our identity in God. How else are we to shred ourselves of the identity we have formed in the world and put on the identity of Jesus Christ? We are to crucify our flesh in order to accomplish this. Crucify means to literally kill our flesh, those things that bring us pleasure outside of the Will of God for humanity.

Fasting is a practical Spiritual discipline. Jesus goes on to further instruct His disciples not to have a sad face while fasting. Don't draw attention to yourself in an effort for someone to ask what is wrong giving you an opportunity to boast about fasting. Jesus told His disciples to literally wash their faces and moisturize them. When we fast we are not to appear as if we are fasting, but instead we should look good and intact like we would any other day. When we fast it is not an opportunity for us to look so worn and distressed. Anything God asks us to do for our sakes is to bring us joy. We are strengthened when we fast. The Glory (God's Power and Presence) of God is with us, in us, and empowering us.

God will openly reward us for our secret sacrifices. The thing about successfully completing a fast is that, only you and God will know. It is not a badge of honor that we were outwardly, but because we do it in secret, God will bless our lives in a way that the our family, friends, community, and even the world will take notice.

Practical Ways To Approach Biblical Fasting

As a novice, I could not for the life of me, wrap my head around the concept of fasting. I needed to know who, what, when, where, and always how. Finally, one day the Holy Spirit spoke to me and simplified it for me. He told me that in order to fast I just needed to not eat or drink anything. I was instructed to pray and read His Word as much as possible during my own set time of fasting and that He (God) would take care of the rest. So, I did just that. One day I decided not to eat in order to Honor God and hear from God. For me, because of my eating pattern, I would not eat from the moment I woke up (around five (5) a.m.) all the way through my lunch hour. For me I couldn't justify fasting up until lunch, when I normally would only eat then. So, again, I decided not to eat until one (1) o'clock pm. This meant that at twelve (12) o'clock pm, I would go out to my car to pray and read the word of God for one hour uninterrupted. Give myself enough time to stop by the cafeteria at work to grab a snack and be back at my desk and not eating until one (1) o'clock pm. I had successfully completed an eight (8) hour fast. From there I would gradually begin to fast for longer periods of time, working my up to a full twenty-four (24) hour fast. The first twenty-four (24) hour fast was excruciating. I didn't have headaches, but I had one major large headache for the full 24 hours that seemingly ran throughout my body. I was constantly talking myself out of being crazy and this task being impossible. We can do anything that we put our spirits to in Christ. Fasting is not impossible and it is rewarding. I now fast at least once during the week from six (6) o'clock a.m. to around three (3) o'clock p.m.. This is roughly the time that our Lord and Savoir was being tried, punished, and crucified before He utter the Powerful words, "It Is Finished.". I'm not saying that this time is a highly divine time and I'm not saying that it is not either. I say that because Acts chapter 10 illustrates that Cornelius was fasting and praying until the ninth (9) hour which is the three (3) o'clock pm hour. Around this hour Cornelius heard from Heaven and received instructions that would not only bless his entire household, but also everyone in his home at the time.

Fasting is not complicated, but God Honors us for doing the simplest of things. Remember, to successfully complete a fast:

1. Do not eat or drink
2. Do it to the Glory, Honor, and Knowledge of God alone
3. Spend time as much as possible in the Presence of God
4. Be rinsed and repeat

IX. The Ultimate List of Fasting Scriptures

Here you will find a list of every scripture in the Bible that fasting is found in. Though every scripture is not listed in its context, they are a great point of reference to start your own personal Biblical study on Living The Fast Life.

1. Judges 20:26 - Then all the children of Israel, that is, all the people, went up and came to the house of God and wept. They sat there before the Lord and fasted that day until evening; and they offered burnt offerings and peace offerings before the Lord.

2. 1 Samuel 7:6 - So they gathered together at Mizpah, drew water, and poured it out before the Lord. And they fasted that day, and said there, "We have sinned against the Lord." And Samuel judged the children of Israel at Mizpah.

3. 1 Samuel 31:13 - Then they took their bones and buried them under the tamarisk tree at Jabesh, and fasted seven days.

4. 2 Samuel 1:12 - And they mourned and wept and fasted until evening for Saul and for Jonathan his son, for the people of the Lord and for the house of Israel, because they had fallen by the sword.

5. 2 Samuel 12:16 - David therefore pleaded with God for the child, and David fasted and went in and lay all night on the ground.

6. 2 Samuel 12:21 - Then his servants said to him, "What is this that you have done? You fasted and wept for the child while he was alive, but when the child died, you arose and ate food."

7. 2 Samuel 12:22 - And he said, "While the child was alive, I fasted and wept; for I said, 'Who can tell whether the Lord will be gracious to me, that the child may live?"

8. 2 Samuel 12:23 - But now he is dead; why should I fast? Can I bring him back again? I shall go to him, but he shall not return to me."

9. 1 Kings 21:9 - She wrote in the letters, saying, Proclaim a fast, and seat Naboth with high honor among the people;

10. 1 Kings 21:12 - They proclaimed a fast, and seated Naboth with high honor among the people.

11. 1 Kings 21:27 - So it was, when Ahab heard those words, that he tore his clothes and put sackcloth on his body, and fasted and lay in sackcloth, and went about mourning.

12. 1 Chronicles 10:12 - all the valiant men arose and took the body of Saul and the bodies of his sons; and they brought them to Jabesh,

and buried their bones under the tamarisk tree at Jabesh, and fasted seven days.

13. 2 Chronicles 20:3 - And Jehoshaphat feared, and set himself to seek the Lord, and proclaimed a fast throughout all Judah.

14. Ezra 8:21 - Then I proclaimed a fast there at the river of Ahava, that we might humble ourselves before our God, to seek from Him the right way for us and our little ones and all our possessions.

15. Ezra 8:23 - So we fasted and entreated our God for this, and He answered our prayer.

16. Ezra 9:5 - At the evening sacrifice I arose from my fasting; and having torn my garment and my robe, I fell on my knees and spread out my hands to the Lord my God.

17. Nehemiah 1:4 - So it was, when I heard these words, that I sat down and wept, and mourned for many days; I was fasting and praying before the God of heaven.

18. Nehemiah 9:1 - Now on the twenty-fourth day of this month the children of Israel were assembled with fasting, in sackcloth, and with dust on their heads.

19. Esther 4:3 - And in every province where the king's command and decree arrived, there was great mourning among the Jews, with fasting, weeping, and wailing; and many lay in sackcloth and ashes.

20. Esther 4:16 - "Go, gather all the Jews who are present in Shushan, and fast for me; neither eat nor drink for three days, night or day. My maids and I will fast likewise. And so I will go to the king, which is against the law; and if I perish, I perish!"

21.	Esther 9:31 - to confirm these days of Purim at their appointed time, as Mordecai the Jew and Queen Esther had prescribed for them, and as they had decreed for themselves and their descendants concerning matters of their fasting and lamenting.

22.	Psalm 35:13 - But as for me, when they were sick, My clothing was sackcloth; I humbled myself with fasting; And my prayer would return to my own heart.

23.	Psalm 69:10 - When I wept and chastened my soul with fasting, That became my reproach.

24.	Psalm 109:24 - My knees are weak through fasting, And my flesh is feeble from lack of fatness.

25.	Isaiah 58:1 - "Cry aloud, spare not; Lift up your voice like a trumpet; Tell My people their transgression, And the house of Jacob their sins.

26.	Isaiah 58:3 - 'Why have we fasted,' they say, 'and You have not seen? Why have we afflicted our souls, and You take no notice?' "In fact, in the day of your fast you find pleasure, And exploit all your laborers.

27.	Isaiah 58:4 - Indeed you fast for strife and debate, And to strike with the fist of wickedness. You will not fast as you do this day, To make your voice heard on high.

28.	Isaiah 58:5 - Is it a fast that I have chosen, A day for a man to afflict his soul? Is it to bow down his head like a bulrush, And to spread out sackcloth and ashes? Would you call this a fast, And an acceptable day to the Lord?

29.	Isaiah 58:6 - "Is this not the fast that I have chosen: To loose the bonds of wickedness, To undo the heavy burdens, To let the oppressed go free, And that you break every yoke?

30.	Jeremiah 14:12 - When they fast, I will not hear their cry; and when they offer burnt offering and grain offering, I will not accept them. But I will consume them by the sword, by the famine, and by the pestilence."

31.	Jeremiah 36:6 - You go, therefore, and read from the scroll which you have written at my instruction, the words of the Lord, in the hearing of the people in the Lord's house on the day of fasting. And you shall also read them in the hearing of all Judah who come from their cities.

32.	Jeremiah 36:9 - Now it came to pass in the fifth year of Jehoiakim the son of Josiah, king of Judah, in the ninth month, that they proclaimed a fast before the Lord to all the people in Jerusalem, and to all the people who came from the cities of Judah to Jerusalem.

33.	Daniel 6:18 - Now the king went to his palace and spent the night fasting; and no musicians were brought before him. Also his sleep went from him.

34.	Daniel 9:3 - Then I set my face toward the Lord God to make request by prayer and supplications, with fasting, sackcloth, and ashes.

35.	Joel 1:14 - Consecrate a fast, Call a sacred assembly; Gather the elders And all the inhabitants of the land Into the house of the Lord your God, And cry out to the Lord.

36.	Joel 2:12- "Now, therefore," says the Lord, "Turn to Me with all your heart, With fasting, with weeping, and with mourning."

37.	Joel 2:15 - Blow the trumpet in Zion, Consecrate a fast, Call a sacred assembly;

38.   Jonah 3:5 - So the people of Nineveh believed God, proclaimed a fast, and put on sackcloth, from the greatest to the least of them.

39.   Zechariah 7:3 - and to ask the priests who were in the house of the Lord of hosts, and the prophets, saying, "Should I weep in the fifth month and fast as I have done for so many years?"

40.   Zechariah 7:5 - "Say to all the people of the land, and to the priests: 'When you fasted and mourned in the fifth and seventh months during those seventy years, did you really fast for Me—for Me?

41.   Zechariah 8:19 - "Thus says the Lord of hosts: 'The fast of the fourth month, The fast of the fifth, The fast of the seventh, And the fast of the tenth, Shall be joy and gladness and cheerful feasts For the house of Judah. Therefore love truth and peace.'

42.   Matthew 4:2 - And when He had fasted forty days and forty nights, afterward He was hungry.

43.   Matthew 6:16 - "Moreover, when you fast, do not be like the hypocrites, with a sad countenance. For they disfigure their faces that they may appear to men to be fasting. Assuredly, I say to you, they have their reward.

44.   Matthew 6:17 - But you, when you fast, anoint your head and wash your face,

45.   Matthew 6:18 - so that you do not appear to men to be fasting, but to your Father who is in the secret place; and your Father who sees in secret will reward you openly.

46.   Matthew 9:14 - Then the disciples of John came to Him, saying, "Why do we and the Pharisees fast often, but Your disciples do not fast?"

47.   Matthew 9:15 - And Jesus said to them, "Can the friends of the bridegroom mourn as long as the bridegroom is with them? But the days will come when the bridegroom will be taken away from them, and then they will fast.

48.   Matthew 17:21 - However, this kind does not go out except by prayer and fasting."

49.   Mark 2:18 - The disciples of John and of the Pharisees were fasting. Then they came and said to Him, "Why do the disciples of John and of the Pharisees fast, but Your disciples do not fast?"

50.   Mark 2:19 - And Jesus said to them, "Can the friends of the bridegroom fast while the bridegroom is with them? As long as they have the bridegroom with them they cannot fast.

51.   Mark 2:20 - But the days will come when the bridegroom will be taken away from them, and then they will fast in those days.

52.   Mark 9:29 - So He said to them, "This kind can come out by nothing but prayer and fasting."

53.   Luke 2:37 - and this woman was a widow of about eighty-four years, who did not depart from the temple, but served God with fastings and prayers night and day.

54.   Luke 5:33 - Then they said to Him, "Why do the disciples of John fast often and make prayers, and likewise those of the Pharisees, but Yours eat and drink?"

55.   Luke 5:34 - And He said to them, "Can you make the friends of the bridegroom fast while the bridegroom is with them?

56.   Luke 5:35 - But the days will come when the bridegroom will be taken away from them; then they will fast in those days."

57.   Luke 18:12 - I fast twice a week; I give tithes of all that I possess.'

58.   Acts 10:30 - So Cornelius said, "Four days ago I was fasting until this hour; and at the ninth hour I prayed in my house, and behold, a man stood before me in bright clothing,

59.   Acts 13:2 - As they ministered to the Lord and fasted, the Holy Spirit said, "Now separate to Me Barnabas and Saul for the work to which I have called them."

60.   Acts 13:3 - Then, having fasted and prayed, and laid hands on them, they sent them away.

61.   Acts 14:23 - So when they had appointed elders in every church, and prayed with fasting, they commended them to the Lord in whom they had believed.

62.   Acts 27:9 - Now when much time had been spent, and sailing was now dangerous because the Fast was already over, Paul advised them,

63.   1 Corinthians 7:5 - Do not deprive one another except with consent for a time, that you may give yourselves to fasting and prayer; and come together again so that Satan does not tempt you because of your lack of self-control.

64.   2 Corinthians 6:5 - in stripes, in imprisonments, in tumults, in labors, in sleeplessness, in fastings;

65.   2 Corinthians 11:27 - in weariness and toil, in sleeplessness often, in hunger and thirst, in fastings often, in cold and nakedness

www.ingramcontent.com/pod-product-compliance
Lightning Source LLC
Chambersburg PA
CBHW061331250726
48657CB00003B/1110